# Table of Contents

# REGIONAL THREATS

# GLOBAL THREATS

## CYBER

We are in a major transformation because our critical infrastructures, economy, personal lives, and even basic understanding of—and interaction with—the world are becoming more intertwined with digital technologies and the Internet. In some cases, the world is applying digital technologies faster than our ability to understand the security implications and mitigate potential risks.

State and nonstate actors increasingly exploit the Internet to achieve strategic objectives, while many governments—shaken by the role the Internet has played in political instability and regime change—seek to increase their control over content in cyberspace. The growing use of cyber capabilities to achieve strategic goals is also outpacing the development of a shared understanding of norms of behavior, increasing the chances for miscalculations and misunderstandings that could lead to unintended escalation.

Compounding these developments are uncertainty and doubt as we face new and unpredictable cyber threats. In response to the trends and events that happen in cyberspace, the choices we and other actors make in coming years will shape cyberspace for decades to come, with potentially profound implications for US economic and national security.

In the United States, we define cyber threats in terms of **cyber attacks** and **cyber espionage**. A cyber attack is a non-kinetic offensive operation intended to create physical effects or to manipulate, disrupt, or delete data. It might range from a denial-of-service operation that temporarily prevents access to a website, to an attack on a power turbine that causes physical damage and an outage lasting for days. Cyber espionage refers to intrusions into networks to access sensitive diplomatic, military, or economic information.

### Increasing Risk to US Critical Infrastructure

We judge that there is a remote chance of a major cyber attack against US critical infrastructure systems during the next two years that would result in long-term, wide-scale disruption of services, such as a regional power outage. The level of technical expertise and operational sophistication required for such an attack—including the ability to create physical damage or overcome mitigation factors like manual overrides—will be out of reach for most actors during this time frame. Advanced cyber actors—such as **Russia** and **China**—are unlikely to launch such a devastating attack against the United States outside of a military conflict or crisis that they believe threatens their vital interests.

However, isolated state or nonstate actors might deploy less sophisticated cyber attacks as a form of retaliation or provocation. These less advanced but highly motivated actors could access some poorly protected US networks that control core functions, such as power generation, during the next two years, although their ability to leverage that access to cause high-impact, systemic disruptions will probably be limited. At the same time, there is a risk that unsophisticated attacks would have significant outcomes due to unexpected system configurations and mistakes, or that vulnerability at one node might spill over and contaminate other parts of a networked system.

- Within the past year, in a denial-of-service campaign against the public websites of multiple US banks and stock exchanges, actors flooded servers with traffic and prevented some customers from accessing their accounts via the Internet for a limited period, although the attacks did not alter customers' accounts or affect other financial functions.

- In an August 2012 attack against Saudi oil company Aramco, malicious actors rendered more than 30,000 computers on Aramco's business network unusable. The attack did not impair production capabilities.

## Eroding US Economic and National Security

Foreign intelligence and security services have penetrated numerous computer networks of US Government, business, academic, and private sector entities. Most detected activity has targeted unclassified networks connected to the Internet, but foreign cyber actors are also targeting classified networks. Importantly, much of the nation's critical proprietary data are on sensitive but unclassified networks; the same is true for most of our closest allies.

- We assess that highly networked business practices and information technology are providing opportunities for foreign intelligence and security services, trusted insiders, hackers, and others to target and collect sensitive US national security and economic data. This is almost certainly allowing our adversaries to close the technological gap between our respective militaries, slowly neutralizing one of our key advantages in the international arena.

- It is very difficult to quantify the value of proprietary technologies and sensitive business information and, therefore, the impact of economic cyber espionage activities. However, we assess that economic cyber espionage will probably allow the actors who take this information to reap unfair gains in some industries.

## Information Control and Internet Governance

Online **information control** is a key issue among the United States and other actors. However, some countries, including Russia, China, and Iran, focus on "cyber influence" and the risk that Internet content might contribute to political instability and regime change. The United States focuses on cyber security and the risks to the reliability and integrity of our networks and systems. This is a fundamental difference in how we define cyber threats.

The current multi-stakeholder model of Internet governance provides a forum for governments, the commercial sector, academia, and civil society to deliberate and reach consensus on Internet organization and technical standards. However, a movement to reshape Internet governance toward a national government-based model would contradict many of our policy goals, particularly those to protect freedom of expression and the free flow of online information and ensure a free marketplace for information technology products and services.

- These issues were a core part of the discussions as countries negotiated a global telecommunications treaty in Dubai in December. The contentious new text that resulted led many countries, including the United States, not to sign the treaty because of its language on network security, spam control, and expansion of the UN's role in Internet governance. The negotiations demonstrated that disagreements on these issues will be long-running challenges in bilateral and multilateral engagements.

Internet governance revision based on the state-management model could result in international regulations over online content, restricted exchange of information across borders, substantial slowdown of technical innovation, and increased opportunities for foreign intelligence and surveillance operations on the Internet in the near term.

## Other Actors

We track cyber developments among nonstate actors, including terrorist groups, hacktivists, and cyber criminals. We have seen indications that some **terrorist organizations** have heightened interest in developing offensive cyber capabilities, but they will probably be constrained by inherent resource and organizational limitations and competing priorities.

**Hacktivists** continue to target a wide range of companies and organizations in denial-of-service attacks, but we have not observed a significant change in their capabilities or intentions during the last year. Most hacktivists use short-term denial-of-service operations or expose personally identifiable information held by target companies, as forms of political protest. However, a more radical group might form to inflict more systemic impacts—such as disrupting financial networks—or accidentally trigger unintended consequences that could be misinterpreted as a state-sponsored attack.

**Cybercriminals** also threaten US economic interests. They are selling tools, via a growing black market, that might enable access to critical infrastructure systems or get into the hands of state and nonstate actors. In addition, a handful of **commercial companies** sell computer intrusion kits on the open market. These hardware and software packages can give governments and cybercriminals the capability to steal, manipulate, or delete information on targeted systems. Even more companies develop and sell professional-quality technologies to support cyber operations—often branding these tools as lawful-intercept or defensive security research products. Foreign governments already use some of these tools to target US systems.

# TERRORISM and TRANSNATIONAL ORGANIZED CRIME

## Terrorism

Terrorist threats are in a transition period as the global jihadist movement becomes increasingly decentralized. In addition, the Arab Spring has generated a spike in threats to US interests in the region that likely will endure until political upheaval stabilizes and security forces regain their capabilities. We also face uncertainty about potential threats from Iran and Lebanese Hizballah, which see the United States and Israel as their principal enemies.

### Evolving Homeland Threat Landscape

*Al-Qa'ida in the Arabian Peninsula (AQAP).* Attacks on US soil will remain part of AQAP's transnational strategy; the group continues to adjust its tactics, techniques and procedures for targeting the West. AQAP leaders will have to weigh the priority they give to US plotting against other internal and regional objectives, as well as the extent to which they have individuals who can manage, train, and deploy operatives for US operations.

***Al-Qa'ida-Inspired Homegrown Violent Extremists (HVE).*** Al-Qa'ida-inspired HVEs—whom we assess will continue to be involved in fewer than 10 domestic plots per year—will be motivated to engage in violent action by global jihadist propaganda, including English-language material, such as AQAP's *Inspire* magazine; events in the United States or abroad perceived as threatening to Muslims; the perceived success of other HVE plots, such as the November 2009 attack at Fort Hood, Texas, and the March 2012 attacks by an al-Qa'ida-inspired extremist in Toulouse, France; and their own grievances. HVE planning in 2012 was consistent with tactics and targets seen in previous HVE plots and showed continued interest in improvised explosive devices (IED) and US Department of Defense (DoD) targets.

***Core Al-Qa'ida***. Senior personnel losses in 2012, amplifying losses and setbacks since 2008, have degraded core al-Qa'ida to a point that the group is probably unable to carry out complex, large-scale attacks in the West. However, the group has held essentially the same strategic goals since its initial public declaration of war against the United States in 1996, and to the extent that the group endures, its leaders will not abandon the aspiration to attack inside the United States.

**The Global Jihadist Threat Overseas: Affiliates, Allies, and Sympathizers**

In 2011, al-Qa'ida and its affiliates played little or no role in the uprisings in the Middle East and North Africa and, with the exception of AQAP, were not well positioned to take advantage of events. At the same time, the rise of new or transitional governments in Egypt, Tunisia, Yemen, and Libya, and ongoing unrest in Syria and Mali, have offered opportunities for established affiliates, aspiring groups, and like-minded individuals to conduct attacks against US interests. Weakened or diminished counterterrorism capabilities, border control mechanisms, internal security priorities, and other shortcomings in these countries—combined with anti-US grievances or triggering events—will sustain the threats to US interests throughout the region. The dispersed and decentralized nature of the terrorist networks active in the region highlights that the threat to US and Western interests overseas is more likely to be unpredictable. The 2012 attack on the US facilities in Benghazi, Libya, and the 2013 attack on Algeria's In-Amenas oil facility demonstrate the threat to US interests from splinter groups, ad hoc coalitions, or individual terrorists who can conduct anti-US operations, even in the absence of official direction or guidance from leaders of established al-Qa'ida affiliates.

- **Al-Qa'ida in Iraq's (AQI)** goals inside Iraq will almost certainly take precedence over US plotting, but the group will remain committed to al-Qa'ida's global ideology. Since the 2011 withdrawal of US forces, AQI has conducted nearly monthly, simultaneous, coordinated country-wide attacks against government, security, and Shia civilian targets. AQI's Syria-based network, the Nusrah Front, is one of the best organized and most capable of the Sunni terrorist groups.

- Somalia-based **al-Shabaab** will remain focused on local and regional challenges, including its longstanding leadership rivalries and its fights against forces from the Somali and Ethiopian Governments and the African Union Mission in Somalia (AMISOM). The group will probably also continue to plot attacks designed to weaken regional adversaries, including targeting US and Western interests in East Africa.

- **Al-Qa'ida in the Land of the Islamic Maghreb's (AQIM)** intentions and capability remain focused on local, US, and Western interests in north and west Africa.

- Nigeria-based **Boko Haram** will continue to select targets for attacks to destabilize the country and advance its extreme vision of Islamist rule.

- Pakistan-based **Lashkar-e-Tayibba (LT)** will continue to be the most multifaceted and problematic of the Pakistani militant groups. The group has the long-term potential to evolve into a permanent and even HAMAS/Hizballah-like presence in Pakistan.

## Iran and Lebanese Hizballah

The failed 2011 plot against the Saudi Ambassador in Washington shows that Iran may be more willing to seize opportunities to attack in the United States in response to perceived offenses against the regime. Iran is also an emerging and increasingly aggressive cyber actor. However, we have not changed our assessment that Iran prefers to avoid direct confrontation with the United States because regime preservation is its top priority.

Hizballah's overseas terrorist activity has been focused on Israel—an example is the Bulgarian Government's announcement that Hizballah was responsible for the July 2012 bus bombing at the Burgas airport that killed five Israeli citizens. We continue to assess that the group maintains a strong anti-US agenda but is reluctant to confront the United States directly outside the Middle East.

# Transnational Organized Crime

Transnational organized crime (TOC) networks erode good governance, cripple the rule of law through corruption, hinder economic competitiveness, steal vast amounts of money, and traffic millions of people around the globe. (Cybercrime, an expanding for-profit TOC enterprise, is addressed in the Cyber section.) TOC threatens US national interests in a number of ways:

*Drug Activity.* Drug trafficking is a major TOC threat to the United States and emanates primarily from the Western Hemisphere. Mexico is the dominant foreign producer of heroin, marijuana, and methamphetamines for the US market. Colombia produces the overwhelming majority of the cocaine that reaches the United States, although the amount of cocaine available to US consumers has substantially decreased in the past five years due to Colombian eradication and security efforts, US transit zone interdiction and capacity-building activities, and warfare among Mexican trafficking organizations. However, high US demand—still twice that of Europe—the capacity of Colombia's remaining drug trafficking organizations, and weak penal and judicial institutions suggest that Colombia's decades-long struggle with the drug threat will continue for a number of years. In addition to the threat inside the United States, the drug trade undermines US interests abroad; for example, it erodes stability in West and North Africa and remains a significant source of revenue for the Taliban in Afghanistan.

*Facilitating Terrorist Activity.* The Intelligence Community is monitoring the expanding scope and diversity of "facilitation networks," which include semi-legitimate travel experts, attorneys, and other types of professionals, as well as corrupt officials, who provide support services to criminal and terrorist groups.

*Money Laundering.* The scope of worldwide money laundering is subject to significant uncertainty but measures more than a trillion dollars annually, often exploiting governments' difficulties coordinating law enforcement across national boundaries. Criminals' reliance on the US dollar also exposes the US financial system to illicit financial flows. Inadequate anti-money laundering regulations, lax enforcement of existing ones, misuse of front companies to obscure those responsible for illicit flows, and new forms of electronic money challenge international law enforcement efforts.

*Corruption.* Corruption exists at some level in all countries; however, the interaction between government officials and TOC networks is particularly pernicious in some countries. Among numerous examples, we assess that Guinea-Bissau has become a narco-state, where traffickers use the country as a transit hub with impunity; and in Russia, the nexus among organized crime, some state officials, the intelligence services, and business blurs the distinction between state policy and private gain.

*Human Trafficking.* President Obama recently noted that upwards of 20 million human beings are being trafficked around the world. The US State Department and our law enforcement organizations have led US Government efforts against human trafficking, and the Intelligence Community has increased collection and analytic efforts to support law enforcement and the interagency Human Smuggling and Trafficking Center. Virtually every country in the world is a source, transit point, and/or destination for individuals being trafficked.

- For example, in 2012 a Ukrainian National was sentenced to life-plus-20-years in prison for operating a human trafficking organization that smuggled young Ukrainians into the United States. For seven years, he and his brothers arranged to move unsuspecting immigrants through Mexico into the United States. With debts of $10,000 to $50,000, victims were forced to live in squalid conditions, enslaved, and subjected to rape, beatings, and other forms of physical attack. Threats against their families in Ukraine were used to dissuade them from attempting to escape.

*Environmental Crime.* Illicit trade in wildlife, timber, and marine resources constitutes a multi-billion dollar industry annually, endangers the environment, and threatens to disrupt the rule of law in important countries around the world. These criminal activities are often part of larger illicit trade networks linking disparate actors—from government and military personnel to members of insurgent groups and transnational organized crime organizations.

# WMD PROLIFERATION

Nation-state efforts to develop or acquire weapons of mass destruction (WMD) and their delivery systems constitute a major threat to the security of our nation, deployed troops, and allies. The Intelligence Community is focused on the threat and destabilizing effects of nuclear proliferation, proliferation of chemical and biological warfare (CBW)-related materials, and development of WMD delivery systems.

Traditionally, international agreements and diplomacy have deterred most nation-states from acquiring biological, chemical, or nuclear weapons, but these constraints may be of less utility in preventing terrorist groups from doing so. The time when only a few states had access to the most dangerous technologies is past. Biological and chemical materials and technologies, almost always dual-use, move easily in our globalized economy, as do the personnel with scientific expertise to design and use them. The latest discoveries in the life sciences also diffuse globally and rapidly.

**Iran and North Korea Developing WMD-Applicable Capabilities**

We assess **Iran** is developing nuclear capabilities to enhance its security, prestige, and regional influence and give it the ability to develop nuclear weapons, should a decision be made to do so. We do not know if Iran will eventually decide to build nuclear weapons.

Tehran has developed technical expertise in a number of areas—including uranium enrichment, nuclear reactors, and ballistic missiles—from which it could draw if it decided to build missile-deliverable nuclear weapons. These technical advancements strengthen our assessment that Iran has the scientific, technical, and industrial capacity to eventually produce nuclear weapons. This makes the central issue its political will to do so.

Of particular note, Iran has made progress during the past year that better positions it to produce weapons-grade uranium (WGU) using its declared facilities and uranium stockpiles, should it choose to do so. Despite this progress, we assess Iran could not divert safeguarded material and produce a weapon-worth of WGU before this activity is discovered.

We judge Iran's nuclear decisionmaking is guided by a cost-benefit approach, which offers the international community opportunities to influence Tehran. Iranian leaders undoubtedly consider Iran's security, prestige and influence, as well as the international political and security environment, when making decisions about its nuclear program. In this context, we judge that Iran is trying to balance conflicting objectives. It wants to advance its nuclear and missile capabilities and avoid severe repercussions—such as a military strike or regime threatening sanctions.

We judge Iran would likely choose a ballistic missile as its preferred method of delivering a nuclear weapon, if one is ever fielded. Iran's ballistic missiles are capable of delivering WMD. In addition, Iran has demonstrated an ability to launch small satellites, and we grow increasingly concerned that these technical steps—along with a regime hostile toward the United States and our allies—provide Tehran with the means and motivation to develop larger space-launch vehicles and longer-range missiles, including an intercontinental ballistic missile (ICBM).

Iran already has the largest inventory of ballistic missiles in the Middle East, and it is expanding the scale, reach, and sophistication of its ballistic missile arsenal. Iran's growing ballistic missile inventory and its domestic production of anti-ship cruise missiles (ASCM) and development of its first long-range land attack cruise missile provide capabilities to enhance its power projection. Tehran views its conventionally armed missiles as an integral part of its strategy to deter—and if necessary retaliate against—forces in the region, including US forces.

**North Korea**'s nuclear weapons and missile programs pose a serious threat to the United States and to the security environment in East Asia, a region with some of the world's largest populations, militaries, and economies. North Korea's export of ballistic missiles and associated materials to several countries, including Iran and Syria, and its assistance to Syria's construction of a nuclear reactor, destroyed in 2007, illustrate the reach of its proliferation activities. Despite the Six-Party Joint Statements issued in 2005 and 2007, in which North Korea reaffirmed its commitment not to transfer nuclear materials, technology, or know-how, we remain alert to the possibility that North Korea might again export nuclear technology.

North Korea announced on 12 February that it conducted its third nuclear test. It has also displayed what appears to be a road-mobile ICBM and in December 2012 placed a satellite in orbit using its Taepo Dong 2 launch vehicle. These programs demonstrate North Korea's commitment to develop long-range missile technology that could pose a direct threat to the United States, and its efforts to produce and market ballistic missiles raise broader regional and global security concerns.

Because of deficiencies in their conventional military forces, North Korean leaders are focused on deterrence and defense. The Intelligence Community has long assessed that, in Pyongyang's view, its nuclear capabilities are intended for deterrence, international prestige, and coercive diplomacy. We do not know Pyongyang's nuclear doctrine or employment concepts. Although we assess with low confidence that the North would only attempt to use nuclear weapons against US forces or allies to preserve the Kim regime, we do not know what would constitute, from the North's perspective, crossing that threshold.

### WMD Security in Syria

We assess **Syria** has a highly active chemical warfare (CW) program and maintains a stockpile of sulfur mustard, sarin, and VX. We assess that Syria has a stockpile of munitions—including missiles, aerial bombs, and possibly artillery rockets—that can be used to deliver CW agents. Syria's overall CW program is large, complex, and geographically dispersed, with sites for storage, production, and preparation. This advanced CW program has the potential to inflict mass casualties, and we assess that an increasingly beleaguered regime, having found its escalation of violence through conventional means inadequate, might be prepared to use CW against the Syrian people. In addition, groups or individuals in Syria could gain access to CW-related materials. The United States and our allies are monitoring Syria's chemical weapons stockpile.

Based on the duration of Syria's longstanding biological warfare (BW) program, we judge that some elements of the program may have advanced beyond the research and development stage and may be capable of limited agent production. Syria is not known to have successfully weaponized biological agents in an effective delivery system, but it possesses conventional and chemical weapon systems that could be modified for biological agent delivery.

# COUNTERINTELLIGENCE

Foreign intelligence services, along with terrorist groups, transnational criminal organizations, and other nonstate actors, are targeting and acquiring our national security information, undermining our economic and technological advantages, and seeking to influence our national policies and processes covertly. These foreign intelligence efforts employ traditional methods of espionage and, with growing frequency, innovative technical means. Among significant foreign threats, **Russia** and **China** remain the most capable and persistent intelligence threats and are aggressive practitioners of economic espionage against the United States. Countering such foreign intelligence threats is a top priority for the Intelligence Community for the year ahead. Moreover, vulnerabilities in global supply chains open opportunities for adversaries to exploit US critical infrastructure. (For a discussion of cyber espionage, see the Cyber section.)

**Threats to US Government Supply Chains**

The US and other national economies have grown more dependent on global networks of supply chains. These web-like relationships, based on contracts and subcontracts for component parts, services, and manufacturing, obscure transparency into those supply chains. Additionally, reliance on foreign equipment, combined with a contracting pool of suppliers in the information technology, telecommunications, and energy sectors, creates opportunities for exploitation of, and increased impact on, US critical infrastructures and systems.

Interdependence of information technologies and integration of foreign technology in US information technology, telecommunications, and energy sectors will increase the potential scope and impact of foreign intelligence and security services' supply chain operations. The likely continued consolidation of infrastructure suppliers—which means that critical infrastructures and networks will be built from a more limited set of provider and equipment options—will also increase the scope and impact of potential supply chain subversions.

# COUNTERSPACE

Space systems and their supporting infrastructures enable a wide range of services, including communication; position, navigation, and timing; intelligence, surveillance, and reconnaissance; and meteorology, which provide vital national, military, civil, scientific, and economic benefits. Other nations recognize these benefits to the United States and seek to counter the US strategic advantage by pursuing capabilities to deny or destroy our access to space services. Threats to vital US space services will increase during the next decade as disruptive and destructive counterspace capabilities are developed. In 2007, China conducted a destructive antisatellite test. In a 2009 press article, a senior Russian military leader stated that Moscow was developing counterspace capabilities.

# NATURAL RESOURCES: INSECURITY and COMPETITION

Competition and scarcity involving natural resources—food, water, minerals, and energy—are growing security threats. Many countries important to the United States are vulnerable to natural resource shocks that degrade economic development, frustrate attempts to democratize, raise the risk of regime-threatening instability, and aggravate regional tensions. Extreme weather events (floods, droughts, heat waves) will increasingly disrupt food and energy markets, exacerbating state weakness, forcing human migrations, and triggering riots, civil disobedience, and vandalism. Criminal or terrorist elements can exploit any of these weaknesses to conduct illicit activity and/or recruitment and training. Social disruptions are magnified in growing urban areas where information technology transmits grievances to larger—often youthful and unemployed—audiences, and relatively "small" events can generate significant effects across regions or the world.

## Food

Natural food-supply disruptions, due to floods, droughts, heat waves, and diseases, as well as policy choices, probably will stress the global food system in the immediate term, resulting in sustained volatility in global food prices. Policy choices can include export bans; diversions of arable lands for other uses,

9

such as urban development; and foreign land leases and acquisitions. Many resource-strapped countries have been losing confidence in the global marketplace to supply vital resources, and increasingly looking to shield their populations in ways that will almost certainly threaten global food production. For example, emerging powers and Gulf States are buying up arable and grazing land around the world as hedges against growing domestic demand and strained resources. Food supplies are also at risk from plant diseases that affect grain and oilseed crops and from transmittable animal diseases, such as H5N1 and foot and mouth disease. At the same time, agricultural inputs—water, fertilizer, land, and fuel oil—are becoming more scarce and/or costly, exacerbating the upward pressure on food prices.

In the coming year, markets for agricultural commodities will remain tight, due in part to drought and crop failures in the midwestern United States last summer. Rising demand for biofuels and animal feed exerts particular pressures on corn prices, and extreme weather will cause episodic deficits in production. We will also see growing demand and high price volatility for wheat. Significant wheat production occurs in water-stressed and climate-vulnerable regions in Asia, where markets will remain susceptible to harvest shocks. A near-term supply disruption could result when a plant disease known as Ug99 stem rust—already spreading across Africa, Asia, and the Middle East—arrives in South Asia, which is likely to happen within the next few years. Wheat production is growing in Eastern Europe, but output is variable, and governments have demonstrated a readiness to impose export controls.

Although food-related state-on-state conflict is unlikely in the near term, the risk of conflict between farmers and livestock owners—often in separate states—will increase as population growth and crop expansion infringe on livestock grazing areas, especially in sub-Saharan Africa and Central Asia. Disputes over fisheries are also likely to increase as water scarcity emerges in major river basins, and marine fisheries are depleted. Shrinking marine fisheries—for example, in the South China Sea—will lead to diplomatic disputes as fishermen are forced to travel further from shore. In addition, government grants of state-owned land to domestic and foreign agricultural developers are likely to stoke conflict in areas without well-defined land ownership laws and regulations.

Terrorists, militants, and international crime organizations can use declining local food security to promote their own legitimacy and undermine government authority. Growing food insecurity in weakly governed countries could lead to political violence and provide opportunities for existing insurgent groups to capitalize on poor conditions, exploit international food aid, and discredit governments for their inability to address basic needs. In addition, intentional introduction of a livestock or plant disease might be a greater threat to the United States and the global food system than a direct attack on food supplies intended to kill humans.

## Water

Risks to freshwater supplies—due to shortages, poor quality, floods, and climate change—are growing. These forces will hinder the ability of key countries to produce food and generate energy, potentially undermining global food markets and hobbling economic growth. As a result of demographic and economic development pressures, North Africa, the Middle East, and South Asia face particular difficulty coping with water problems.

Lack of adequate water is a destabilizing factor in countries that do not have the management mechanisms, financial resources, or technical ability to solve their internal water problems. Some states are further stressed by heavy dependence on river water controlled by upstream nations with unresolved water-sharing issues. Wealthier developing countries probably will experience increasing water-related social disruptions, although they are capable of addressing water problems without risk of state failure.

Historically, water tensions have led to more water-sharing agreements than violent conflicts. However, where water-sharing agreements are ignored, or when infrastructure development—for electric power generation or agriculture—is seen as a threat to water resources, states tend to exert leverage over their neighbors to preserve their water interests. This leverage has been applied in international forums and has included pressuring investors, nongovernmental organizations, and donor countries to support or halt water infrastructure projects. In addition, some nonstate terrorists or extremists will almost certainly target vulnerable water infrastructure to achieve their objectives and continue to use water-related grievances as recruitment and fundraising tools.

Many countries are using groundwater faster than aquifers can replenish in order to satisfy food demand. In the long term, without mitigation actions (drip irrigation, reduction of distortive electricity-for-water pump subsidies, access to new agricultural technology, and better food distribution networks), exhaustion of groundwater sources will cause food demand to be satisfied through increasingly stressed global markets.

Water shortages and pollution will also harm the economic performance of important US trading partners. Economic output will suffer if countries do not have sufficient clean water to generate electrical power or to maintain and expand manufacturing and resource extraction. In some countries, water shortages are already having an impact on power generation, and frequent droughts are undermining long-term plans to increase hydropower capacity. With climate change, these conditions will continue to deteriorate.

## Minerals: China's Monopoly on Rare Earth Elements

Rare earth elements (REE) are essential to civilian and military technologies and to the 21st century global economy, including development of green technologies and advanced defense systems. China holds a commanding monopoly over world REE supplies, controlling about 95 percent of mined production and refining. China's dominance and policies on pricing and exports are leading other countries to pursue mitigation strategies, but those strategies probably will have only limited impact within the next five years and will almost certainly not end Chinese REE dominance. REE prices spiked after China enacted a 40-percent export quota cut in July 2010, peaking at record highs in mid-2011. As of December 2012, REE prices had receded but still remained at least 80 percent, and as much as 600 percent (depending on the type of REE), above pre-July 2010 levels.

Mines in Australia, Brazil, Canada, Malawi, the United States, and Vietnam are expected to be operational in less than five years. However, even as production at non-Chinese mines come online, initial REE processing outside of China will remain limited because of technical difficulties, regulatory hurdles, and capital costs associated with the startup of new or dormant processing capabilities and facilities. China will also continue to dominate production of the most scarce and expensive REEs, known as heavy REEs, which are critical to defense systems.

## Energy

Oil prices will remain highly sensitive to political instability in the Middle East, tensions with Iran, and global economic growth. In 2012 increasing US, Iraqi, and Libyan output, combined with slow economic growth, helped ease upward pressure on prices. In the coming year, most growth in new production probably will come from North America and Iraq, while production from some major producers stagnates or declines because of policies that discourage investment.

Sustained oil prices above $80 per barrel would support the growth in North American oil production. That growth is being propelled by the production of tight oil, due to the application of horizontal drilling and hydrolic fracturing. Many Organization of the Petroleum Exporting Countries (OPEC) members are increasingly dependent on high oil prices to support government spending. However, the budgets of countries that subsidize domestic fuel consumption will come under greater stress with high oil prices and rising domestic demand.

Natural gas prices will remain regionally based, with North American consumers probably paying one-third the price of European importers and one-fourth that of Asian consumers. With the prospects for US liquefied natural gas (LNG) exports made possible by the growth in shale gas production, along with other global LNG exports, major European and Asian importers probably will continue to pressure their suppliers to de-link their prices from oil. Weather, economic indicators, and energy policies in Japan probably will have the strongest influence on global LNG prices. Australia is poised to become a top LNG exporter but faces project cost inflation that could slow development.

## Climate Change and Demographics

Food security has been aggravated partly because the world's land masses are being affected by weather conditions outside of historical norms, including more frequent and extreme floods, droughts, wildfires, tornadoes, coastal high water, and heat waves. Rising temperature, for example, although enhanced in the Arctic, is not solely a high-latitude phenomenon. Recent scientific work shows that temperature anomalies during growing seasons and persistent droughts have hampered agricultural productivity and extended wildfire seasons. Persistent droughts during the past decade have also diminished flows in the Nile, Tigris-Euphrates, Niger, Amazon, and Mekong river basins.

Demographic trends will also aggravate the medium- to long-term outlooks for resources and energy. Through roughly 2030, the global population is expected to rise from 7.1 billion to about 8.3 billion; the size of the world's population in the middle class will expand from the current 1 billion to more than 2 billion; and the proportion of the world's population in urban areas will grow from 50 percent to about 60 percent—all putting intense pressure on food, water, minerals, and energy.

# HEALTH and PANDEMIC THREATS

Scientists continue to discover previously unknown pathogens in humans that made the "jump" from animals—zoonotic diseases. Examples are: a prion disease in cattle that jumped in the 1980s to cause variant Creutzeldt-Jacob disease; a bat henipavirus that in 1999 became known as the human Nipah Virus; a bat corona virus that jumped to humans in 2002 to cause Severe Acute Respiratory Syndrome (SARS); and another SARS-like corona virus recently identified in individuals who have been in Saudi

Arabia, which might also have bat origins. Human and livestock population growth and encroachment into jungles increase human exposure to crossovers. No one can predict which pathogen will be the next to spread to humans, or when or where such a development will occur, but humans will continue to be vulnerable to pandemics, most of which will probably originate in animals.

An easily transmissible, novel respiratory pathogen that kills or incapacitates more than one percent of its victims is among the most disruptive events possible. Such an outbreak would result in a global pandemic that causes suffering and death in every corner of the world, probably in fewer than six months. This is not a hypothetical threat. History is replete with examples of pathogens sweeping populations that lack immunity, causing political and economic upheaval, and influencing the outcomes of wars—for example, the 1918 Spanish flu pandemic affected military operations during World War I and caused global economic disruptions.

The World Health Organization has described one influenza pandemic as "the epidemiological equivalent of a flash flood." However, slow-spreading pathogens, such as HIV/AIDS, have been just as deadly, if not more so. Such a pathogen with pandemic potential may have already jumped to humans somewhere; HIV/AIDS entered the human population more than 50 years before it was recognized and identified. In addition, targeted therapeutics and vaccines might be inadequate to keep up with the size and speed of the threat, and drug-resistant forms of diseases, such as tuberculosis, gonorrhea, and Staphylococcus aureus, have already emerged.

## MASS ATROCITIES

Mass atrocities continue to be a recurring feature of the global landscape. Most of the time they occur in the context of major instability events. Since the turn of the last century, hundreds of thousands of civilians have lost their lives as a result of atrocities occurring during conflicts in the Darfur region of Sudan and in the eastern Congo (Kinshasa). Recent atrocities in Syria, where tens of thousands of civilians have lost their lives within the past two years, have occurred against a backdrop of major political upheaval, illustrating how most mass atrocities tend to be perpetrated by ruling elites or rebels who use violence against civilians to assert or retain control. Consistent with this trend, mass atrocities also are more likely in places where governments discriminate against minorities, socioeconomic conditions are poor, or local powerbrokers operate with impunity. In addition, terrorists and insurgents might exploit such conditions to conduct attacks against civilians, as in Boko Haram's attacks on churches in Nigeria. Less frequently, violence between sectarian or ethnic groups can create the conditions for mass atrocities.

# REGIONAL THREATS

## MIDDLE EAST and NORTH AFRICA

### Arab Spring

Although some countries have made progress towards democratic rule, most are experiencing uncertainty, violence, and political backsliding. The toppling of leaders and weakening of regimes have also unleashed destabilizing ethnic and sectarian rivalries. Islamist actors have been the chief electoral beneficiaries of the political openings, and Islamist parties in Egypt, Tunisia and Morocco will likely solidify their influence in the coming year. The success of transitioning states will depend, in part, on their ability to integrate these actors into national politics and to integrate—or marginalize—political, military, tribal, and business groups that were part of or benefitted from the old regimes. At the same time, transitions that fail to address public demands for change are likely to revive unrest and heighten the appeal of authoritarian or extremist solutions.

Three issues, in particular, will affect US interests:

- *Ungoverned Spaces.* The struggles of new governments in places like Tripoli and Sanaa to extend their writs, as well as the worsening internal conflict in Syria, have created opportunities for extremist groups to find ungoverned space from which to destabilize the new governments and prepare attacks against Western interests inside those countries.

- *Economic Hardships.* Many states face economic distress—specifically, high rates of unemployment—that is unlikely to be alleviated by current levels of Western aid and will require assistance from wealthy Arab countries as well as reforms and pro-growth policies. Failure to meet heightened popular expectations for economic improvement could set back transitions in places such as Egypt and destabilize vulnerable regimes such as Jordan. Gulf states provide assistance only incrementally and are wary of new governments' foreign policies and their ability to absorb funds.

- *Negative Views of the United States.* Some transitioning governments are more skeptical than their predecessors about cooperating with the United States and are concerned about protecting sovereignty and resisting foreign interference. This has the potential to hamper US counterterrorism efforts and other initiatives to engage transitioning governments.

### Egypt

Since his election in June 2012, Egyptian President Muhammad Mursi has worked to consolidate control of the instruments of state power and loosen the Egyptian military's grip on the government. Mursi has taken actions that have advanced his party's agenda and his international reputation, including his late-2012 role brokering a HAMAS-Israeli cease-fire. However, his decree in November 2012 that temporarily increased his authorities at the expense of the judiciary angered large numbers of Egyptians—especially secular activists—and brought protesters back to the streets.

Quelling popular dissatisfaction and building popular support for his administration and policies are critical for Mursi and will have a direct bearing on the Freedom and Justice Party's success in upcoming parliamentary elections. A key element of Mursi's ability to build support will be improving living standards and the economy; GDP growth fell to 1.5 percent in 2012 from just over 5 percent in 2010, and unemployment was roughly 12.6 percent in mid-2012.

# Syria

Almost two years into the unrest in Syria, we assess that the erosion of the Syrian regime's capabilities is accelerating. Although the Asad regime has prevented insurgents from seizing key cities—such as Damascus, Aleppo, and Homs—it has been unable to dislodge them from these areas. Insurgent forces also have been gaining strength in rural areas of northern and eastern Syria, particularly Idlib Province along the border with Turkey, where their progress could lead to a more permanent base for insurgent operations. Prolonged instability is also allowing al-Qa'ida's Nusrah Front to establish a presence within Syria. (For details on Syria's weapons and chemical and biological warfare programs, see the Proliferation section.)

- Sanctions and violence have stifled trade, commercial activity, and foreign investment, and reduced the regime's financial resources—as many as 2.5 million people are internally displaced and roughly 700,000 have fled to neighboring countries since March 2011. The Syrian economy contracted by 10 to 15 percent in 2012, which has forced the regime to prioritize security spending and cut back on providing basic services, food and fuel, and health and education services for the public.

# Iran

Iran is growing more autocratic at home and more assertive abroad as it faces elite and popular grievances, a deteriorating economy, and an uncertain regional dynamic. Supreme Leader Khamenei's power and authority are now virtually unchecked, and security institutions, particularly the Islamic Revolutionary Guard Corps (IRGC), have greater influence at the expense of popularly elected and clerical institutions. Khamenei and his allies will have to weigh carefully their desire to control the 14 June Iranian presidential election, while boosting voter turnout to increase the appearance of regime legitimacy and avoid a repeat of the disputed 2009 election. Meanwhile, the regime is adopting more oppressive social policies to increase its control over the population, such as further limiting educational and career choices for women.

Iran's financial outlook has worsened since the 2012 implementation of sanctions on its oil exports and Central Bank. Iran's economy contracted in 2012 for the first time in more than two decades. Iran's access to foreign exchange reserves held overseas has diminished, and preliminary data suggest that it suffered its first trade deficit in 14 years. Meanwhile, the rial reached an all-time low in late January, with the exchange rate falling from about 15,000 rials per dollar at the beginning of 2012 to nearly 40,000 rials per dollar, and inflation and unemployment are growing.

Growing public frustration with the government's socioeconomic policies has not led to widespread political unrest because of Iranians' pervasive fear of the security services and the lack of effective opposition organization and leadership. To buoy the regime's popularity and forestall widespread civil unrest, Iranian leaders are trying to soften the economic hardships on the poorer segments of the population. Khamenei has publicly called on the population to pursue a "resistance economy," reminiscent of the hardships that Iran suffered immediately after the Iranian Revolution and during the Iran-Iraq war. However, the willingness of contemporary Iranians to withstand additional economic austerity is unclear because most Iranians do not remember those times; 60 percent of the population was born after 1980 and 40 percent after 1988.

In its efforts to spread influence abroad and undermine the United States and our allies, Iran is trying to exploit the fighting and unrest in the Arab world. It supports surrogates, including Palestinian militants engaged in the recent conflict with Israel. To take advantage of the US withdrawals from Iraq and Afghanistan, it will continue efforts to strengthen political and economic ties with central and local governments, while providing select militants with lethal assistance. Iran's efforts to secure regional hegemony, however, have achieved limited results, and the fall of the Asad regime in Syria would be a major strategic loss for Tehran. (For details on Iran's weapons programs, see the Proliferation section.)

## Iraq

Since the US departure, the Iraqi Government has remained generally stable, with the major parties pursuing change through the political process rather than violence. However, there are rising tensions between Prime Minister Maliki and Kurdistan Regional Government President Masud Barzani and an increase in anti-regime Sunni protests since the end of 2012. Maliki is pressing for greater authority over disputed territories in northern Iraq, and Barzani is pushing forward to export hydrocarbons independent of Baghdad.

AQI conducted more vehicle and suicide bombings in 2012 than in 2011, almost exclusively against Iraqi targets. However, AQI and other insurgent groups almost certainly lack sufficient strength to overwhelm Iraqi Security Forces, which has put pressure on these groups through arrests of key individuals.

Iraq is producing and exporting oil at the highest levels in two decades, bolstering finances for a government that derives 90 to 95 percent of its revenue from oil exports. Iraq increased production capacity from about 2.4 million barrels per day in 2010 to roughly 3.3 million barrels per day in 2012. However, it is still wrestling with the challenges of diversifying its economy and providing essential services.

## Yemen

We judge that Yemen's new president, Abd Rabuh Mansur Hadi, has diminished the power of former President Salih and his family and kept the political transition on track, but Salih's lingering influence, AQAP's presence, and the tenuous economy are significant challenges. Yemen's humanitarian situation is dire, with nearly half of the population considered "food insecure." Obtaining foreign aid and keeping its oil pipeline open will be crucial to Sanaa's potential economic improvement. The next key political milestone will be the successful completion of an inclusive National Dialogue that keeps Yemen on course for elections in 2014, although some southern leaders are threatening non-participation. Hadi's government will also have to maintain pressure on AQAP following a military offensive this past summer that displaced the group from its southern strongholds.

## Lebanon

Lebanon's stability will remain fragile during the next year primarily because of the tensions triggered by the Syrian conflict. We expect Lebanon will be able to avoid destabilizing sectarian violence, but it is likely to experience occasional, localized clashes between pro- and anti-Asad sectarian militias. Thus far, political leaders have succeeded in muting popular outrage over the October 2012 bombing that killed a popular Sunni figure, and the Lebanese Armed Forces remain effective at controlling small-scale violence.

## Libya

Libya's leaders are struggling to rebuild after the revolution and the collapse of the Qadhafi regime. The institutional vacuum caused by Qadhafi's removal increased terrorist activity and gave rise to hundreds of well-armed regional militias, many of which played key roles in overthrowing the regime but now complicate Libya's stability. The transitional government is struggling to control the militias, but it remains reliant on some to provide security in the absence of cohesive and capable security institutions. Eastern Libya has been traditional hubs of extremists, and if left unchecked by Libyan authorities and allied militias, groups operating from there could pose a recurring threat to Western interests.

The government is also working to rebuild its administrative capacity as it manages the post-revolutionary transition and is overseeing the drafting of a constitution, which will set the stage for elections as soon as this year. Libya has quickly resumed high levels of oil production, which is critical to rebuilding the economy. As of late 2012, it restored crude oil output to near preconflict levels of 1.6 million barrels per day, but Tripoli will need the expertise and support of international oil companies to sustain, if not boost, overall supply.

# SOUTH ASIA

## Afghanistan

The upcoming presidential election is scheduled for April 2014, while the International Security Assistance Force (ISAF) is completing its drawdown.

We assess that the Taliban-led insurgency has diminished in some areas of Afghanistan but remains resilient and capable of challenging US and international goals. Taliban senior leaders also continue to be based in Pakistan, which allows them to provide strategic guidance to the insurgency without fear for their safety. Al-Qa'ida's influence on the insurgency is limited, although its propaganda gains from participating in insurgent attacks far outweigh its actual battlefield impact.

Security gains are especially fragile in areas where ISAF surge forces have been concentrated since 2010 and are now transitioning the security lead to Afghan National Security Forces (ANSF). The ANSF will require international assistance through 2014 and beyond. The Afghan National Army and Afghan National Police have proven capable of providing security in major cities, nearby rural areas, and key ground lines of communication in the vicinity of government-controlled areas. The Afghan Air Force has made very little progress. The National Directorate of Security remains Afghanistan's premier national intelligence service and likely will play a larger role in regime security over time.

In addition, Afghanistan's economy, which has been expanding at a steady rate, is likely to slow after 2014. Kabul has little hope of offsetting the coming drop in Western aid and military spending, which have fueled growth in the construction and services sectors. Its licit agricultural sector and small businesses have also benefited from development projects and assistance from nongovernmental organizations, but the country faces high rates of poverty, unemployment, food insecurity, and poppy cultivation.

## Pakistan

Pakistan is preparing for national and provincial assembly elections, which must be held no later than May 2013, and a presidential election later in the year. Pakistani officials note that these elections are a milestone—the first time a civilian government has completed a five-year term and conducted a transfer to a new government through the electoral process.

Islamabad is intently focused on Afghanistan in anticipation of the ISAF drawdown. The Pakistani Government has attempted to improve relations with Kabul and ensure that its views are taken into consideration during the transition period. The military this year continued operations in the Federally Administered Tribal Areas (FATA) and, as of late 2012, had forces in place for an operation against anti-Pakistan militants in the North Waziristan Agency of the FATA. There were fewer domestic attacks by the Tehrik-eTaliban Pakistan this year than in the previous several years.

Economically, trouble looms. Pakistan, with its small tax base, poor system of tax collection, and reliance on foreign aid, faces no real prospects for sustainable economic growth. The government has been unwilling to address economic problems that continue to constrain economic growth. The government has made no real effort to persuade its disparate coalition members to accept much-needed policy and tax reforms, because members are focused on retaining their seats in upcoming elections. Sustained remittances from overseas Pakistanis (roughly $13 billion from July 2011 to June 2012, according to Pakistan's central bank) have helped to slow the loss of reserves. However, Pakistan has to repay the IMF $1.7 billion for the rest of this fiscal year for money borrowed as part of its 2008 bailout agreement; growth was around 3.5 percent in 2012; and foreign direct investment and domestic investment have both declined substantially.

## India

Both India and Pakistan have made calculated decisions to improve ties, despite deep-rooted mistrust. They held a series of meetings in the past year and will probably continue to achieve incremental progress on economic relations, such as trade, while deferring serious discussion on the more contentious issues of territorial disputes and terrorism. Even modest progress, however, could easily be undone by a terrorist attack against India linked to Pakistan, which could trigger a new crisis and prompt New Delhi to freeze bilateral dialogue.

India will continue to support the current Afghan Government to ensure a stable and friendly Afghanistan. India furthered its engagement with Afghanistan in 2012 and signed an additional four memoranda of understanding on mining, youth affairs, small development projects, and fertilizers during President Karzai's visit to New Delhi in November 2012. We judge that India sees its goals in Afghanistan as consistent with US objectives, and favors sustained ISAF and US presence in the country. India will almost certainly cooperate with the United States and Afghanistan in bilateral and multilateral frameworks to identify assistance activities that will help bolster civil society, develop capacity, and strengthen political structures in Afghanistan. Moreover, India consistently ranks in the top three nations that Afghans see as helping their country rebuild. As of April 2012, India ranked as Afghanistan's fifth largest bilateral donor.

Neither India nor China currently seeks to overturn the strategic balance on the border or commit provocations that would destabilize the relationship. However, India and China are each increasing their military abilities to respond to a border crisis. Both consider these moves to be defensive, but they are probably fueling mutual suspicion and raising the stakes in a potential crisis. As a result, periodic, low-level intrusions between forces along the border could escalate if either side saw political benefit in more forcefully and publicly asserting its territorial claims or responding more decisively to perceived aggression. However, existing mechanisms, as well as a shared desire for stability by political and military leaders from both sides, will likely act as an effective break against escalation.

# AFRICA

Throughout Africa, violence, corruption, and extremism pose challenges to US interests in 2013. As in 2012, Africa's stability will be threatened not only by unresolved discord between Sudan and South Sudan, fighting in Somalia, and extremist attacks in Nigeria, but also by the collapse of governance in northern Mali and renewed conflict in the Great Lakes region. Elsewhere, African countries are vulnerable to political crises, democratic backsliding, and natural disasters. On the positive side, in parts of the continent, development is advancing—for example, in Ghana—and, in Somalia, international efforts and domestic support are widening areas of tenuous stability.

## Sudan and South Sudan

**Sudan**'s President Bashir and the National Congress Party (NCP) are confronting a range of challenges, including public dissatisfaction over economic decline and insurgencies on Sudan's southern and western borders. Sudanese economic conditions have deteriorated since South Sudan's independence, when South Sudan took control of the majority of oil reserves. The country now faces a decline in economic growth that jeopardizes political stability and fuels opposition to Bashir and the NCP. Khartoum is likely to resort to heavy-handed tactics to prevent protests from escalating and will pursue a military response to provocations by Sudan People's Liberation Movement-North (SPLM-N) rebels in Southern Kordofan and Blue Nile States. An uptick in violence in Sudan's western Darfur region toward the end of the rainy season in October 2012 will probably continue through 2013. Islamist extremists remain active in Sudan potentially threatening the security of the Sudanese Government as well as US and other Western interests.

**South Sudan** in 2013 will face issues that threaten to destabilize its fragile, untested, poorly resourced government. Festering ethnic disputes are likely to undermine national cohesion, and the southern government will struggle to provide security, manage rampant corruption, and deliver basic services. Despite a series of agreements in the wake of Juba's incursion into Sudan in April 2012, controversial unresolved disputes, such as the future of Abyei, risk a return to conflict between the two countries. Animosity and lack of trust between Khartoum and Juba also threaten to undermine the implementation of agreements signed in September 2012. South Sudan's economy suffered significant setbacks after Juba shut down oil production in early 2012, and it will struggle to rebound because unresolved security conflicts with Sudan have delayed the restart of oil production, despite a signed deal with Khartoum in September 2012. Ethnic conflict in South Sudan is likely to continue as the South Sudanese military struggles to disarm ethnic militias and provide security across the country. We assess the ruling Sudan People's Liberation Movement (SPLM) will continue to turn to the international community, specifically the United States, for assistance.

## Somalia

Somalia's political transition in 2012 installed new political players and degraded the influence of old guard politicians responsible for corruption and mismanagement of government resources under the transitional government system. The country's nascent institutions, ill-equipped to provide social services, along with pervasive technical, political, and administrative challenges at the national level, will test Mogadishu's ability to govern effectively in 2013. Command and control of AMISOM forces and their proxies, along with facilitating cooperation between Mogadishu and AMISOM forces operating in southern Somalia, will also be distinct challenges for the government.

Al-Shabaab, the al-Qa'ida-affiliated insurgency that has terrorized populations and destabilized the transitional government since 2008, is largely in retreat, ameliorating instability and opening space for legitimate governing entities to exert control in southern Somalia. Despite its fractious state, al-Shabaab continues to plan attacks in Somalia and has returned to launching asymmetric attacks in a meager attempt to reassert control in key areas, including Mogadishu and the port city of Kismaayo. The group also poses a threat to US and Western interests in Somalia and regionally, particularly in Kenya, and leverages its operatives and networks in these locales for attacks.

## Mali

In January 2012, after the return of heavily armed Tuareg fighters from Libya, the secular-based National Movement for the Liberation of the Azawad (MNLA) and the extremist Islamist Tuareg rebel group Ansar al-Din launched a rebellion against the Malian Government. Following a 21 March military coup, Ansar al-Din—with help from AQIM—and the MNLA quickly drove the Malian military out of the north. After taking control of northern Mali, AQIM worked closely with Ansar al-Din and AQIM-offshoot Movement for Tawhid and Jihad in West Africa (TWJWA) to consolidate gains in the region and impose a hard-line version of sharia.

Armed conflict between Malian Armed Forces and Islamist forces renewed in early 2013 when Islamist forces attacked Malian military outposts near Islamist-held territory. French forces quickly intervened with ground forces and airstrikes, halting AQIM and its allies' advances and eventually pushing them out of key northern Malian population centers. Regional forces and Chadian troops have begun to deploy to Mali, where European Union trainers will begin the training cycle of designated forces. Several countries have now offered significant contributions to the deploying force but lack adequate troops, training, and logistics to provide a capable force.

Mali's fragile interim government faces an uphill effort to reunite the country and hold democratic elections by mid-2013—especially elections the north perceives as credible. In addition to planning elections, local and regional actors are pursuing diplomatic options, including negotiations, to address instability in northern Mali and counter AQIM's influence.

## Nigeria

The Nigerian state is acutely challenged by uneven governance, endemic corruption, inadequate infrastructure, weak health and education systems, and recurring outbreaks of sectarian, ethnic, and communal violence. Abuja also faces Boko Haram—a northern Sunni extremist group with ties to AQIM—whose attacks on Christians and fellow Muslims in Nigeria have heightened religious and ethnic tensions and raised concerns of possible attacks against US interests in the country. Communal violence is down from last year, but Boko Haram has made moves to incite it, and the Nigerian Government is scarcely addressing the underlying causes, such as socioeconomic conditions in troubled northern Nigeria, despite pledges to do so. In the Niger Delta, Abuja is struggling to extricate itself from open-ended financial commitments and has not made progress rehabilitating, retraining, and reintegrating disgruntled former militants. Militant/criminal attacks on land-based oil infrastructure in Nigeria's coastal areas, along with hijackings, kidnappings, and piracy attacks off the coast, continue at a steady pace.

## Central Africa

The **Great Lakes** region of Central Africa has a total population of 128 million and includes parts or all of Burundi, Congo (Kinshasa), and Uganda. Despite gains in peace and security in the past decade, the region endures the chronic pressures of weak governance, ethnic cleavages, and active rebel groups. US Government-sponsored modeling suggests that Burundi, Congo (Kinshasa), and Uganda are all at risk of violent instability during the next year. Rwandan-backed M23 rebels in Eastern Congo in 2012 engaged the Armed Forces of Congo and UN peacekeepers in the worst fighting since 2008, displacing more than a quarter-million civilians. Other armed groups will likely increase predatory activity, encouraged by Congolese President Kabila's flawed election in 2011 and his deteriorating control. Several of these nations have become US Government security partners in recent years. Ugandan and Burundian troops compose the vanguard of AMISOM, and Rwanda is a vital part of the peacekeeping mission in Darfur.

Since 2008, Uganda has deployed troops across Congo, South Sudan, and Central African Republic to pursue Joseph Kony and the Lord's Resistance Army (LRA), with US assistance, including approximately 100 US military advisors. While LRA foot soldiers terrorize civilians in the region, Joseph Kony and his top lieutenants evade detection and tracking by keeping low profiles and moving in scattered bands across a remote region.

# EAST ASIA

## China

### Regional Dynamics

During 2012, Beijing adopted strong, uncompromising positions in maritime territorial disputes with several of its neighbors. In each case, China sought to expand its control over the relevant territories and obstructed regional efforts to manage the disputes. Beijing's regional activities appear to be, in part, a response to the US strategic rebalance toward Asia-Pacific, which Chinese leaders believe is aimed at undermining China's position in the region. Globally, Beijing has both assisted and hindered US policy objectives on such issues as Iran, Syria, Afghanistan, and North Korea, and it continues to expand its economic influence and to try to parlay it into greater political influence.

The leadership transition in Beijing continues to unfold as Chinese leaders grapple with a confluence of domestic problems—including lagging economic indicators, corruption, and pressure for political reform—that are fueling leadership fears about the potential for serious domestic unrest.

The leadership team that is confronting these internal challenges is also likely to maintain uncompromising positions on foreign policy issues, especially those involving maritime and territorial disputes in the South and East China Seas. Meanwhile, China-Taiwan relations remained relatively calm in 2012, due in part to the continuity provided by Taiwan President Ma Ying-jeou's reelection last January. However, progress in cross-strait dialogue almost certainly will continue to be gradual, and the cross-strait military and economic balance will keep shifting in China's favor.

## Military Developments

China is pursuing a long-term comprehensive military modernization designed to enable China's armed forces to achieve success on a 21$^{st}$ century battlefield. China's military investments favor capabilities designed to strengthen its nuclear deterrent and strategic strike, counter foreign military intervention in a regional crisis, and provide limited, albeit growing, capacity for power projection. During 2012, China's People's Liberation Army (PLA) introduced advanced weapons into its inventory and reached milestones in the development of key systems, thereby sustaining the modernization program that has been under way since the late 1990s. For example, in August, the PLA Navy commissioned the *Liaoning*, China's first aircraft carrier, which Beijing probably sees as a significant step in developing a military commensurate with great-power status. Additionally, China has continued to develop advanced ballistic missiles.

Developments in Chinese military capabilities support an expansion of PLA operations to secure Chinese interests beyond territorial issues. To expand operations—specifically in the Indian Ocean— China is pursuing more effective logistical support arrangements with countries in the region. Beijing is also maintaining a multi-ship antipiracy task force in the Gulf of Aden for the fourth straight year to protect commercial shipping. The task force operates independently of international efforts, but is making a tangible contribution to protecting shipping through this heavily pirated area.

China is also supplementing its more advanced military capabilities by bolstering maritime law enforcement (MLE) activities in support of its territorial claims in the South and East China Seas. In the territorial disputes with the Philippines and Japan last year, the Chinese Navy stayed over the horizon as MLE vessels provided Beijing's on-scene presence and response.

# North Korea

Kim Jong Un has quickly consolidated power since taking over as leader of North Korea when his father, Kim Jong Il, died in December 2011. Kim has publicly focused on improving the country's troubled economy and the livelihood of the North Korean people, but we have yet to see any signs of serious economic reform.

North Korea maintains a large, conventional military force held in check by the more powerful South Korean-US military alliance. Nevertheless, the North Korean military is well postured to conduct limited attacks with little or no warning, such as the 2010 sinking of a South Korean warship and the artillery bombardment of a South Korean island along the Northern Limit Line. (For information on North Korea's nuclear weapons program and intentions, see the Proliferation section.)

# RUSSIA and EURASIA

## Russia

### Domestic Political Developments

During the next year, Russia's political system of managed democracy will come under greater strain as the Kremlin grapples with growing social discontent and a society that is increasingly in flux. Important sectors of the Russian public are frustrated with the country's sluggish economy and are no longer content with a political system that lacks any real pluralism and suffers from poor and arbitrary governance and endemic corruption. All of these factors present Russian President Vladimir Putin with far greater challenges than any he faced during his two previous terms in office.

Putin's return to the presidency in 2012 was intended to restore strength and vigor to a system that he believed had weakened under President Dmitriy Medvedev. Instead, antipathy over the Putin-Medvedev job swap touched off some of the largest political protests Russia has seen since the breakup of the Soviet Union. Despite these unprecedented protests, the Russian leadership has demonstrated firm resolve to preserve the system, while a disparate opposition movement struggles to become more cohesive, broaden its base, and build momentum. After initially tolerating demonstrations and offering a few political reforms in the hope of dividing the opposition, the Kremlin took a more aggressive approach, adopting measures to restrict opposition activities, such as targeting opposition figures for harassment and using legislative and judicial means to confront, intimidate, and arrest opponents. These actions have helped to thwart the opposition's ability to build momentum and preserve the Kremlin's control of the political system, but they have not addressed the sources of bitterness and dissatisfaction.

### Foreign Policy

Russian foreign policy is unlikely to deviate significantly from its current course in the next year, but domestic political factors almost certainly will exert greater influence on foreign policy. Putin is sensitive to any US criticisms of Russian domestic political practices, which he perceives as meddling in Russia's internal affairs. Nevertheless, he sees benefits in cooperating with the United States on certain issues.

Missile defense will remain a sensitive issue for Russia. Russian leaders are wary that in the long run US pursuit of a "missile shield" will result in systems that enable the United States to undercut Russia's nuclear deterrent and retaliatory capabilities. Russian leaders also see aspects of US plans for missile defense in Europe as serious threats to their core national security interests. The Kremlin will continue to look to the United States and our NATO partners for guarantees that any system will not be directed at Russia. On Syria, Russia is likely to remain a difficult interlocutor. The Kremlin will remain focused on preventing outside military intervention aimed at ousting the Asad regime. Moscow is troubled by the Libyan precedent and believes the West is pursuing a reckless policy of regime change that will destabilize the region and could be used against Russia. The Russians point to the rise of the Muslim Brotherhood in Egypt and the terrorist attacks against US diplomats in Libya last September as evidence supporting their arguments.

Moscow is not likely to change its diplomatic approach to Iran's nuclear program. Russia argues that confidence-building measures and an incremental system of rewards are the best ways to persuade Iran to cooperate with the International Atomic Energy Agency. Despite disagreements over missile defense and the problems of Iran's nuclear program and Syria, Moscow supports US-led NATO military operations in Afghanistan. It sees its support of the Northern Distribution Network (NDN) as a pillar of US-Russia relations that also helps stabilize Afghanistan. Nevertheless, Russia is suspicious of US intentions in Afghanistan and wary of any US efforts to maintain a residual military presence after 2014 without a UN mandate, which could put Moscow's cooperation beyond this period in doubt.

Although the bilateral relationship with the United States will remain important for Russia, Moscow is most likely to focus its foreign policy efforts on strengthening its influence over the states of the former USSR by binding them closer through integration initiatives, such as the Russia-Belarus-Kazakhstan Customs Union or Putin's proposed Eurasian Union.

**The Military**

Russian military forces, both nuclear and conventional, support deterrence and enhance Moscow's geopolitical clout. Since late 2008 the Kremlin has embraced a wide-ranging military reform and modernization program to field a smaller, more mobile, better-trained, and high-tech force during the next decade. This plan represents a radical break with historical Soviet approaches to manpower, force structure, and training. The initial phases, mainly focused on force reorganization and cuts in the mobilization base and officer corps, have been largely implemented and are being institutionalized. The ground forces alone have reduced about 60 percent of armor and infantry battalions since 2008, while the Ministry of Defense cut about 135,000 officer positions, many at field grade.

Moscow is now setting its sights on long-term challenges of rearmament and professionalization. In 2010, a 10-year procurement plan was approved to replace Soviet-era hardware and bolster deterrence with a balanced set of modern conventional, asymmetric, and nuclear capabilities. However, funding, bureaucratic, and cultural hurdles—coupled with the challenge of reinvigorating a military industrial base that deteriorated for more than a decade after the Soviet collapse—complicate Russian efforts.

The reform and modernization programs will yield improvements that will allow the Russian military to more rapidly defeat its smaller neighbors and remain the dominant military force in the post-Soviet space, but they will not—and are not intended to—enable Moscow to conduct sustained offensive operations against NATO collectively. In addition, the steep decline in conventional capabilities since the collapse of the Soviet Union has compelled Moscow to invest significant capital to modernize its conventional forces. At least until Russia's high precision conventional arms achieve practical operational utility, Moscow will embrace nuclear deterrence as the focal point of its defense planning. It still views its nuclear forces as critical for ensuring Russian sovereignty and relevance on the world stage and for offsetting its military weaknesses vis-à-vis potential opponents with stronger militaries.

## The Caucasus and Central Asia

Recent developments in **Georgia,** following the victory of Prime Minister Bidzina Ivanishvili's Georgian Dream party in the October 2012 parliamentary elections, offer new hope for easing bilateral Russian-Georgian tensions. Prime Minister Ivanishvili has expressed interest in normalizing relations with Russia and has sought to improve the tone of the dialogue with Moscow. However, after nearly a decade of President Mikheil Saakashvili's United National Movement party rule, Georgia faces a challenging political transition and an increased risk of domestic political instability.

The standoff between **Armenia** and **Azerbaijan** over the Armenian-occupied Nagorno-Karabakh region remains a potential flashpoint. Heightened rhetoric, distrust on both sides, and recurring violence along the Line of Contact increase the risk of miscalculations that could escalate the situation with little warning.

The threat of instability remains in the states of **Central Asia**. Central Asian leaders have prioritized regime stability over political and economic reforms that could improve long-term governance and legitimacy. Most fear any signs of Arab Spring-type uprisings and repress even small signs of discontent. The Central Asian states have not built constructive relationships with each other; personal rivalries and longstanding disputes over borders, water, and energy create bilateral frictions between neighbors and potential flashpoints for conflict. Ethnic conflicts are also possible and could emerge with little warning. Clashes between ethnic Uzbeks and Kyrgyz in southern Kyrgyzstan following the 2010 overthrow of the government resulted in the deaths of more than 400 people, and in the absence of government efforts to lead reconciliation, tensions between these ethnic groups remain high.

## Ukraine, Belarus, and Moldova

In **Belarus**, Lukashenko has weathered an economic crisis that presented him with the greatest challenge to his rule since he took power in 1994. Corrective measures and financial assistance from Russia have eased some of the more harmful consequences of the crisis, and opposition movements, such as the Revolution through Social Networks, have petered out. Nevertheless, Belarus's economic situation remains precarious, and Lukashenko's refusal to institute structural economic reforms raises the likelihood that Belarus will fall into another economic crisis in 2013.

Under President Yanukovych, **Ukraine** is drifting towards authoritarianism. The October 2012 parliamentary elections were marred by irregularities and fell far short of Western standards for free and fair elections, representing a step backwards from prior Ukrainian elections. Yanukovych also shows few signs that he intends to release imprisoned opposition leader former Prime Minister Yuliya Tymoshenko any time soon, a key condition to improving Ukraine's relations with the West. The government appears to be "doubling down," preparing additional criminal charges against Tymoshenko that could keep her behind bars for life. In addition, the lack of structural economic reforms coupled with a precarious financial situation raises the risk of economic crisis in 2013.

The status quo in **Moldova** is likely to prevail during the next year. Electing new leaders in Moldova and in the separatist region of Transnistria has improved the tone of relations between Chisinau and Tiraspol. A renewed focus on confidence-building measures, such as easing restrictions on the movement of people and goods, generated cautious optimism in early 2012 about progress toward eventual settlement of the Transnistria conflict. However, the negotiating positions of both sides later hardened, and a settlement to the conflict is highly unlikely in the next year.

# LATIN AMERICA and THE CARIBBEAN

Positive trends in much of Latin America include the deepening of democratic principles, economic growth, and resilience in the face of the global financial crisis. Income inequality in the region is also showing a steady decline. In some areas, however, economic stagnation, high rates of violent crime and impunity, ruling party efforts to manipulate democratic institutions to consolidate power, and slow recovery from natural disasters are challenging these strides. Initiatives to strengthen regional integration are leading some countries to try to limit US influence, but they are hampered by ideological differences and regional rivalries.

Iran has been reaching out to Latin America and the Caribbean to decrease its international isolation. President Ahmadinejad traveled to the region twice in 2012. Tehran has cultivated ties to leaders of the Venezuelan-led Alliance for the Peoples of our Americas (ALBA) in Bolivia, Cuba, Ecuador, Nicaragua, and Venezuela, and maintains cordial relations with Cuba and Nicaragua. Relations with Tehran offer these governments a way to stake out independent positions on the international issue of Iran, while extracting financial aid and investment for economic and social projects.

The drug threat to the United States emanates primarily from the Western Hemisphere; the overwhelming majority of drugs now consumed in the United States are produced in Mexico, Colombia, Canada, and the United States. Patterns in drug marketing and trafficking create conditions that could fuel this trend and further undermine citizen security in several countries in the region. Central American governments, especially Honduras, El Salvador and Guatemala, are trying to cope with some of the highest violent crime and homicide rates in the world. In addition, weak and corrupt institutions in these countries foster permissive environments for gang and criminal activity, limit democratic freedom, encourage systemic corruption, and slow recovery.

## Mexico

Recently inaugurated Mexican President Enrique Peña Nieto inherited a complex security situation marked by confrontation between the state and drug cartels, strong public concern over levels of violence, and unprecedented security cooperation with the United States. Peña Nieto has said he will prioritize efforts to reduce violence and push reforms aimed at strengthening the rule of law, including: Mexico's transition to an accusatory system of justice, a more effective counter-illicit finance regime, police professionalization, and bolstered government intelligence capabilities.

President Calderon turned over the presidency to Peña Nieto on 1 December, having made headway against several cartels, in particular Los Zetas, the Beltran Leyva Organization, and the Gulf Cartel. Drug-related homicides have increased significantly since 2007—Calderon's first full year in office—and remain high; more than 50,000 Mexicans have died as a result of drug-related violence since that year.

Peña Nieto promised to push forward Calderon's landmark 2008 constitutional reform to overhaul Mexico's judicial system. The judicial reform process has been uneven across Mexico's states, and many are unlikely to meet the 2016 implementation deadline. On police reform, Peña Nieto plans to create a new gendarmerie, or paramilitary police, to gradually take over policing duties from the military. He also has publicly endorsed efforts to reform and modernize the federal police, as well as state and municipal-level police forces. Peña Nieto's plans to emphasize anti-money laundering efforts will be strengthened by a recently passed law that restricts high-value dollar and peso purchases commonly used to launder drug proceeds, such as in real estate sales, and requires government entities to provide data to support money-laundering prosecutions.

## Venezuela

Venezuelan President Hugo Chavez's death on 5 March has triggered preparations for a new election in which we expect Vice President Nicolas Maduro to compete against Miranda Governor and former presidential candidate Henrique Capriles Radonski. Venezuelan Foreign Minister Elias Jaua announced that Maduro will take over as interim president and that an election will be held within 30 days. Maduro is a long-time Chavez loyalist and will almost certainly continue Chavez's socialist policies.

The Venezuelan Government will be up against the consequences of an increasingly deteriorating business environment and growing macroeconomic imbalances. Debt obligations will consume a growing share of Venezuela's oil revenues, even if oil prices remain high. Lingering citizen concerns that Caracas will face in the next year also include personal safety, which has been threatened by a rising tide of violent crime.

## Cuba

Cuban President Raul Castro is proceeding cautiously with economic reforms to reduce the state's direct role in the economy and diversify trade relations, while preserving socialism and the regime. Measures implemented since 2011 to expand self-employment, permit sales of vehicles and property, and lease state lands to farmers are generally popular but have failed to produce much growth. With their primary patron Hugo Chavez's death, Cuba's leaders are urgently trying to attract foreign investment partners and increase their access to hard currency and foreign credit.

A priority for Cuban leaders is ensuring that economic reform does not increase pressure for a political opening and greater individual rights. There is no indication that Castro's efforts, including his stated interest in laying the groundwork for a generational transition in leadership, will loosen the regime's grip on power. The stiff prison term imposed on USAID subcontractor Alan Gross for facilitating uncensored Internet connectivity demonstrates the Castro regime's sensitivity to public access to technology and information beyond its control. Indeed, harsh government repression of peaceful protests and an upswing in short-term arrests of dissidents indicate economic changes will not be coupled with political changes.

Havana recently announced a new travel and migration policy for most Cubans that will no longer require exit permits and extends the time Cubans can remain abroad without forfeiting property and other rights. The new policy has thus far only prompted a modest boost in US visas. The US Interests Section in Havana recently implemented process improvements that dramatically reduced wait times for non-immigrant visa appointments. Countries around the region are watching for any indication of significant increases in Cuban nationals arriving under the new travel policy, but to date they have seen no such increases.

## Haiti

Stability in Haiti is fragile because of the country's weak governing institutions. Strained relations between President Michel Martelly, in office since May 2011, and the opposition-dominated legislature are delaying progress on several fronts, including plans to hold overdue Senate and local elections and advance the President's agenda to create jobs, improve education, and attract foreign investment. Although Martelly is generally still popular, the risk of social unrest could grow because of unmet expectations over living conditions and the lack of economic opportunities. President Martelly will likely face continued protests—some possibly violent and organized by his enemies—over rising food costs.

President Martelly and Prime Minister Laurent Lamothe intend to prioritize private-sector-led growth and end dependence on aid. However, Haiti will remain dependent on the international community for the foreseeable future because of the devastating effects of the earthquake in January 2010 on infrastructure and production capacity, several recent natural disasters that ruined staple food crops, and the unsettled political and security climate. Of the estimated 1.5 million Haitians displaced by the earthquake, more than 350,000 are still in tent encampments. We assess that the current threat of a mass migration from Haiti is relatively low because Haitians are aware of the standing US policy of rapid repatriation of migrants intercepted at sea.

# EUROPE

## Euro-Zone Crisis

European leaders are still grappling with the euro-zone crisis—the euro zone's economy slipped back into recession in 2012 following two years of slow economic growth. We noted last year that the outcome of the crisis has major implications not just for the United States but also for the world economy. The risk of an unmanaged breakup of the euro zone is lower this year because European Union (EU) leaders have taken steps to strengthen banking and fiscal integration, but economic deterioration in Europe threatens to depress world growth.

This year, rising anger over austerity could affect Europe's social and political fabric. Given high unemployment—particularly among youth—throughout the peripheral euro-zone states (Greece, Italy, Portugal, and Spain), there has been an uptick in strikes and violent protests. The greatest risk to stability is austerity- and reform-fatigue spreading across Europe. In November 2012, tens of thousands marched—mostly in southern Europe but also in Belgium and France—in the first pan-EU labor union action against budget cuts. The crisis has already led most European states to cut defense spending, reducing the capability of Allies to support NATO and other US security interests around the world.

## Turkey

Turkey's activist foreign policy has changed fundamentally during the past year, mostly in reaction to Asad's brutal approach to the opposition-led unrest in Syria. Ankara has since begun to support overtly the Syrian political opposition by hosting its members in Turkey. This is a departure from Turkey's ruling Justice and Development party (AKP)-designed foreign policy approach, which emphasized engagement and incentives for shaping behavior but is now driven by the destabilizing regional effects of the Asad regime's actions. Turkey continues to call on the international community to take action against Asad and is increasingly turning to the United States and NATO for assistance in managing the crisis.

The Turkish Kurdish terrorist group Kurdistan People's Congress (KGK/former PKK) is Ankara's primary security threat. Turkey's Kurdish issue, marked by armed struggle against insurgent KGK forces now entering its fourth decade, is increasingly challenging Ankara domestically with regional implications. KGK-initiated violence inside of Turkey is at its deadliest level in more than a decade. This development is fueling public opposition to much-needed constitutional reforms to address the Turkish Kurdish minority's legitimate demands for political and cultural rights. The sharp rise in violence has pushed Ankara to lean more toward military, vice political, means to deal with the KGK, although efforts are under way to re-launch talks with the KGK leadership. Kurds in Syria are taking advantage of unrest fomented by the opposition to Asad, which is stoking Turkish fears of Kurdish separatism in Turkey.

Turkish relations with Iraq are strained. Turkish leaders are concerned about what they perceive to be increasingly authoritarian tendencies of the Maliki-led government, relations among communities within Iraq, and perceived trends in Iraq's foreign policy. Iraq has been angered by Turkey's efforts to expand political and energy ties with Iraq's semi-autonomous Kurdistan Region without consulting Baghdad.

The Turkey-Israel bilateral relationship remains troubled. In a September 2012 speech, Erdogan said Turkey would not normalize relations with Israel until Israel met Ankara's three conditions: publicly apologizing for the 2010 incident in which Israel interdicted an aid flotilla headed for Gaza and killed nine aboard the ship Mavi Marmara; providing reparations to the families of the Mavi Marmara victims; and lifting the Gaza blockade. Israel's late 2012 operation against HAMAS and other Palestinian militant groups in Gaza further hardened Turkish attitudes. There seem to be few prospects for improving relations between Israel and Turkey.

## The Balkans

Ethnic and internal political divides in the **Western Balkans** will continue to pose the greatest risk to regional stability in 2013. Many fragile states in the region suffer from economic stagnation, high unemployment, corruption, and weak rule of law. Although the security situation in Kosovo's Serb-majority north has improved since fall 2011, Western diplomatic and security engagement is needed to implement many of the agreements reached in EU-sponsored talks.

As the EU-facilitated dialogue to help normalize relations between **Kosovo** and **Serbia** gains traction, the risk of threats and violence by ethnic Serb hardliners in northern Kosovo probably will increase. Serbia gained EU candidacy status in March 2012 and would like a date to begin EU accession talks. However, the relatively new government (elected last May) faces large hurdles in fulfilling EU accession criteria and reconciling Serbia's constitutional claims to Kosovo with the fact that Kosovo is independent. Kosovo's supervised independence ended in September 2012, and Pristina will likely seek to expand its instruments of sovereignty over its territory. The Kosovo Government opened the Mitrovica North Administrative Office in July 2012, extending government services to the Serb-majority region. In June 2013, Kosovo law allows the government to change the mandate of Pristina's potential efforts to transition the Kosovo Security Force (KSF). This warrants attention to avoid negative responses from Belgrade and the Kosovo Serb community in northern Kosovo.

In **Bosnia-Herzegovina** (BiH), differences among Serb, Croat, and Bosniak elites are intensifying, threatening BiH's state institutions and posing obstacles to further Euro-Atlantic integration. A series of political crises have distracted attention from pursuing needed reforms for EU and NATO integration, and secessionist rhetoric from the leadership of the political entity Republika Srpska has further challenged Bosnia's internal cohesion. In **Macedonia**, we do not expect a return to the civil war violence of a decade ago. However, disputes between Albanian and Macedonian communities might become more polarized in the coming year. Tension between Macedonia and **Bulgaria** warrants attention. In addition, Greece's ongoing objection to the country using the name "Macedonia" is another source of friction, and blocks Macedonia's EU and NATO aspirations. In **Albania**, government institutions suffer from corruption and excessive political influence. In the lead-up to the June 2013 parliamentary elections, there is worry about a return to the heated, partisan conflict that erupted after the 2009 parliamentary elections, when the opposition party contested the election and boycotted parliament on-and-off for nearly two years.